The Guitar
King of Strings

By Chip Lovitt

CELEBRATION PRESS

Pearson Learning Group

Contents

The Sound Heard 'Round the World

The sale of the most famous item at a New York City **auction** begins. The bids come faster and faster. By the end of the sale, the item sells for nearly a million dollars.

Just what is the object of such high-priced bids? Is it a prized painting? No, it's a guitar. It's Tiger, a handmade electric guitar that belonged to the musician Jerry Garcia.

Jerry Garcia playing guitar on stage with his band

The sale of Tiger set a record for the highest price ever paid for a guitar. The auction showed that guitars are more than just popular musical instruments. The guitar is now a symbol of modern music. About 14 million Americans play the guitar. There are millions of other guitar players around the world.

Guitars are also pieces of art. They are displayed in some of the world's most famous museums. Rare, old guitars are prized collectors' items. They sell for hundreds of thousands of dollars.

Guitars are big business. In 2002, more than a billion dollars was spent on guitars and guitar accessories. However, the guitar's appeal goes far beyond money and hit songs. Thanks to musicians such as the Beatles and Jimi Hendrix, the guitar has risen above its humble roots.

Since its first appearance, the guitar has had a colorful history. This history is filled with legendary musicians, inventors, and innovators.

Wood + Wires = Sound

There are two kinds of guitars: **acoustic** and electric. Most acoustic guitars have a large hollow body with a round opening, called a **soundhole**. Strings are stretched over the soundhole. When the strings are strummed, they vibrate. These vibrations make sound waves. The sound waves echo inside the guitar and are pushed out through the soundhole. The guitar's body, top, and soundhole act like a loudspeaker.

Acoustic guitar

Acoustic guitars have either steel or nylon strings. Steel-string guitars are often used in rock, pop, and folk music. Nylon-string guitars are also called classical guitars. They are sometimes used to play classical music.

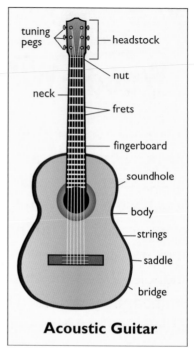

Acoustic Guitar

Most acoustic guitars are made from wood. Different woods vibrate in their own ways and have distinctive sounds. The kinds of woods used to make guitars include ash, maple, and rosewood. Some guitars are made from other products, such as the mineral graphite.

There are two types of electric guitars: **solidbody** and **hollowbody**. Solidbody guitars are made of a solid piece of wood or other material. Hollowbody guitars have a large open chamber, like an acoustic guitar.

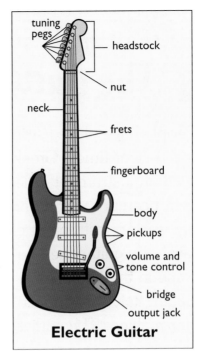

tuning pegs

headstock

nut

neck

frets

fingerboard

body

pickups

volume and tone control

bridge

output jack

Electric Guitar

All electric guitars contain a device called a **pickup**. It acts like a microphone. It turns the strings' vibrations into electrical signals. Then it sends the signals to an **amplifier**. Amplifiers, or amps, enhance the sound of guitars.

Electric guitars are modern instruments. Acoustic guitars have been played for hundreds of years. However, the history of guitars begins thousands of years ago.

The Guitar's Journey

People have played stringed instruments since ancient times. Greeks and Romans played an instrument called a lyre in the seventh century B.C. In the thirteenth century, there was an instrument called a guitarra in Spain. The guitar-like lute was popular in Europe in the late 1400s.

Spain, Italy, and France were early centers of guitar making. The earliest guitars had four or five courses of strings. Each course had two strings. By the 1700s, most guitars were made with six single strings. This is the style for modern guitars.

In the 1800s, Antonio de Torres Jurado was a **luthier**, or maker of guitars, in Spain. He found many ways to improve the guitar's sound. His guitars had a larger body and a louder sound than other guitars at that time. Many of the features that he used are still seen in today's guitars.

In the early 1800s in Vienna, Austria, Johann Stauffer was an expert guitar builder. He made many improvements to the instrument. One of his workers, C. F. Martin, became a famous maker of

A seventeenth-century lute

acoustic guitars in America.

Christian Frederick Martin was born in 1796 in Germany. He learned how to make guitars as a boy. He left home when he was 15 years old and traveled to Vienna. There, he worked for Stauffer. In 1833, Martin traveled to America.

Martin opened a guitar shop in New York City. His guitars were popular, and his business grew. After five years, he moved to Nazareth, Pennsylvania. There he formed C. F. Martin & Company.

Martin's guitars were unique. They were very strong because Martin glued wooden strips under the top of the guitar body. This technique is called X-bracing. It allowed steel strings to be strung on acoustic guitars. Today, X-bracing is still used.

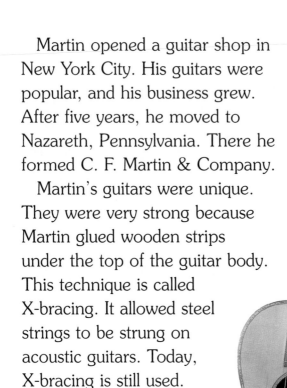

An early nineteenth-century Martin guitar

After C. F. Martin died, his son and grandson continued his work. By the 1920s, the Martin company was making thousands of guitars each year. C. F. Martin IV, the great-great-great grandson of the company founder, runs the business today.

Orville Gibson was another giant of American guitar making. He was born in New York in 1856. Gibson worked in a shoe store. He was also a woodworker and a talented guitar player.

Gibson moved to Michigan in the 1890s. He began making unique guitars. Other guitar makers would bend thin strips of wood to form the curved shapes of a guitar. Gibson carved his guitars out of solid wood. Gibson's guitars were beautiful instruments. Soon, musicians all across America were playing them.

Between 1920 and 1930, bands became popular. Radio was also introduced. This created a boom in guitar sales. America became the guitar-making capital of the world.

Going Electric

In the early 1930s, musicians and inventors were trying to figure out how to combine electricity and guitars. Adolph Rickenbacker and George Beauchamp probably invented the first guitar pickup. They used it to create an early electric guitar. The guitar had a round body and a long neck. It was nicknamed Frying Pan.

Adolph Rickenbacker holding Frying Pan

Other people were also experimenting with electric guitars. In 1936, the Epiphone Company made an electric guitar. They called it the Electar.

Jazz musicians were very interested in electric guitars. Before the 1930s, jazz guitarists played acoustic guitars. It was hard to hear them over the horns and drums in their bands. Electric guitars were loud enough to be heard, even in big bands.

Les Paul, also called "Rhubarb Red," was an electric guitar pioneer. He was a jazz guitarist. Paul decided to make his own electric guitar. He stuck a record player's needle into the top of an acoustic guitar. When Paul played the guitar, the sounds he made were amplified through the record player's speaker.

Around 1940, Paul added strings to a solid piece of wood. He wired it with pickups. Then he cut an acoustic guitar in half and glued the two halves to the wood so it looked like a guitar, his electric guitar. He named this the Log.

Paul worked with the Gibson Company to create a line of guitars. These guitars are still made. They are some of the most popular electric guitars.

The history of another great guitar maker began with country singer Merle Travis. In the late 1940s, Travis asked guitar maker Paul Bigsby to build him a guitar. Bigsby made it out of a solid piece of wood. He never made this kind of guitar for anyone else. Instead, he sent customers to an electronics wizard named Leo Fender.

Legenda
guitarist
Les Paul
playing g

Leo Fender couldn't play a note on the guitar. Yet, he created some of the most popular guitars ever made. Fender built his first acoustic guitar at age 16.

In the late 1930s, Fender started playing with electric guitar pickups. He met many musicians and talked to them about their instruments. By the late 1940s, he and a partner had formed a company that made electric guitars.

Around 1945, Leo Fender started his own company. In 1952, he introduced the Telecaster guitar. It was named after a new invention, the television. It was a simple and dependable solidbody electric guitar. It cost

$189.50. This was a lot of money in 1952.

The Telecaster was criticized by some people. They described it as more like a boat paddle than a musical instrument. Musicians liked it, though. The Telecaster remains a top-selling guitar today.

In 1954, Fender introduced the Stratocaster. The Stratocaster had sleek lines and a modern shape. It would become the guitar of choice for rock musicians like Jimi Hendrix and Bonnie Raitt.

Leo Fender did not invent electric guitars. However, he was the first person to make money mass-producing them. Fender was compared to automobile maker Henry Ford. He made guitars the way Ford produced automobiles: He created high-quality guitars in large numbers.

Fender Stratocaster

Guitar Heroes and the Rise of the Electric Guitar

Les Paul, Leo Fender, and others were involved in the creation of the electric guitar. However, it was musicians who put the instrument in the spotlight. One early guitarist showed what the electric guitar could do. He was a young African American from Oklahoma named Charlie Christian.

Charlie Christian playing guitar

Christian played electric guitar in Benny Goodman's orchestra. His music was a style of jazz called swing. It would have been impossible to play without an amplified electric instrument.

In the 1940s and 1950s, many African Americans from the southern states moved north. They brought rural blues music with them. Blues musicians had played acoustic guitars. They quickly discovered the power and energy of electric guitars.

One of the earliest blues stars was Aaron "T-Bone" Walker. Walker is known as the Father of the Electric Blues. He used his electric guitar to create a swinging mix of blues and jazz. Walker was exciting to watch. He performed wild stage moves such as splits. He also played his guitar behind his back.

In the 1950s, companies like Fender, Gibson, and Epiphone began selling cheap electric guitars. More musicians could afford them. As a result, the electric guitar was heard more often in all kinds of music.

Aaron "T-Bone" Walker giving an exciting stage performance

Many rock stars of the 1950s used electric guitars. Elvis Presley's hits featured the electric guitar. Chuck Berry played rock and roll on his electric guitar. Another early rock star, Buddy Holly, used his Stratocaster to give his songs an unforgettable edge.

In February 1964, a British rock group called the Beatles made their American television debut. Millions of people watched them sing and play their electric guitars. Before long, electric guitars could be heard on the radio all across America.

The Beatles inspired many people to form their own bands. It seemed as if the sound of electric guitars could be heard from every garage and basement. Rock and roll and the electric guitar were here to stay.

There are many rock legends from this time. Eric Clapton and Cream made powerful music. They used electric guitars and loud amps. Other 1960s guitar legends include Jimmy Page of Led Zeppelin and Carlos Santana.

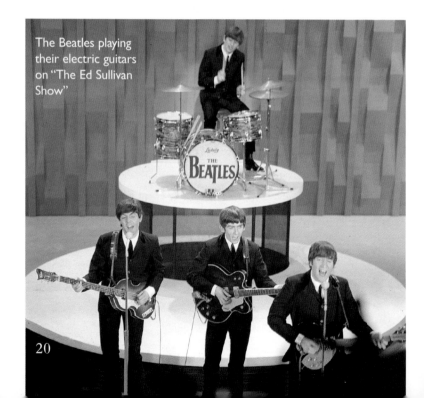

The Beatles playing their electric guitars on "The Ed Sullivan Show"

However, it was Seattle-born Jimi Hendrix who totally changed electric guitar music. Hendrix's style was original. He created a wild mix of guitar sounds that no one had ever heard before. Music would never be the same.

Electric guitar sales boomed in the 1960s and 1970s. Later, guitarists like Stevie Ray Vaughn and Eddie Van Halen created new fans of the instrument. Other performers, such as Bruce Springsteen, Dave Matthews, and Sheryl Crow continue to make the guitar the heart of their music.

Today, there are even more possibilities for the electric guitar. Musicians use guitar **synthesizers** to create new sounds. This type of playing would have been impossible just ten years ago. Synthesizers can make guitars sound like trumpets, harmonicas, or saxophones. A guitar can also be plugged into a computer. Music can be digitally recorded. Then it can be made into a CD by almost anyone.

A Guitar Timeline

1200s–1400s
People play guitarlike instruments, including the lute and guitarra.

1600s
Guitars become popular in parts of Europe.

1770s
Guitars are made with six strings.

1817
Antonio de Torres Jurado is born in Spain.

1833
C. F. Martin comes to America.

1902
Orville Gibson founds his guitar company.

1934
The Frying Pan electric guitar is introduced.

Mid-1930s
Gibson and Epiphone make their first electric guitars.

Early 1940s
Les Paul demonstrates the Log.

Early 1950s
Leo Fender introduces the Telecaster.

1952
Gibson reveals the first Les Paul guitars.

1954
Fender introduces the Stratocaster.

1964
The Beatles appear on "The Ed Sullivan Show."

1960s–1970s
Electric guitar players, such as Jimmy Page, Carlos Santana, and Jimi Hendrix, become popular.

1990s
A new generation of guitarists, including Dave Matthews and Sheryl Crow, makes the guitar the heart of its music.

1970s–1980s
Eddie Van Halen and Stevie Ray Vaughn become famous.

2002
Two of Jerry Garcia's guitars sell for a total of $1.75 million at an auction in New York City.

1996
The Scott Chinery Collection of guitars goes on display at the Smithsonian Institution.

Timeline markers: 1200, 1300, 1400, 1500, 1600, 1700, 1800, 1900, 1910, 1920, 1930, 1940, 1950, 1960, 1970, 1980, 1990, 2000

The World of Vintage Guitars

Today, many old, or vintage, guitars are worth far more than new ones. Guitar collectors and musicians want these vintage guitars. They have a special sound and quality not found in new instruments. "As a well-made wood instrument gets older, it usually gets better and better sounding," says Stan Jay, president of Mandolin Brothers, a vintage guitar shop.

Stan Jay in Mandolin Brothers, a vintage guitar shop

Why do some vintage guitars sound better than new guitars? As a guitar's wood ages, it dries out. The sound also becomes fuller after a guitar has been played for many years. Sound will often echo longer inside an older guitar than in a newer one.

Over time, some vintage guitars become hard to find. When this happens, they become more expensive. "Collectibility," explains Jay, "is based on rarity, supply, and demand."

Some old electric guitars are worth a small fortune today. A Fender Telecaster cost $189.50 in 1952. Today, this guitar sells for more than $15,000. A Fender Stratocaster cost $249.50 in 1954. Today, it can sell for $23,000.

Some Les Paul guitars from 1959 and 1960 had beautiful sunburst "flame-top" finishes. The "flames" came from the wavy patterns of the wood. A Gibson Les Paul sunburst flame-top guitar cost $280 in 1959. Today, some of these guitars are worth $100,000.

Prices of vintage acoustic guitars can also be high. "That 1939 Martin Model D-45 that was $200 then is $150,000 now," says Jay. However, guitars that were owned by celebrities are among the most valuable.

Elvis Presley played 1955 and 1956 Gibson SJ-200s. As a result, they are highly prized. A 1969 Fender Stratocaster that Jimi Hendrix played at the Woodstock music festival sold for $320,000 in 1990. One of Eric Clapton's Fender Stratocasters sold for $497,500!

Jimi Hendrix playing at Woodstock

Some guitars are so rare that they are more than collectors' items. John D'Angelico made handcrafted guitars from 1932 to 1964 in New York City. They are well made, unique, and very hard to find. Buyers often view them as investments. They believe that the value of these guitars will increase.

One of the rarest D'Angelico guitars is a teardrop-shaped New Yorker jazz guitar. It was purchased in 1993 for $150,000. It has been called the world's most collectible guitar.

D'Angelico teardrop-shaped New Yorker jazz guitar from the Chinery Collection

Not all old guitars sell for super-high prices. Some are very affordable. A guitar from the 1960s can cost only a few hundred dollars. There are magazines and Web sites devoted to vintage guitars. They can also be purchased in auctions and in guitar shops.

Museums often have rare instrument collections that include guitars. Recently, the Museum of Fine Arts in Boston displayed more than 100 guitars from the last 400 years.

Another show was at the Smithsonian Institution in Washington, D.C. The Smithsonian Institution displayed Scott Chinery's guitar collection. Chinery was a guitar collector who owned more than 1,000 instruments. Many of Chinery's guitars were treasures or oddities.

Famous guitars are also on display at the Rock and Roll Hall of Fame in Cleveland, Ohio. This display includes guitars owned by Bono of U2, Kurt Cobain, Jimi Hendrix, and Duane Allman.

A Thing for Strings

Guitars are incredibly popular musical instruments. More than 10 million Web sites are devoted to guitars. "The guitar is the only instrument," says Stan Jay, "that allows a beginner to learn just enough music in one hour to accompany himself or herself on more than a thousand songs. Learn just three **chords**, and you can play everything from 'On Top of Old Smokey' to Johnny Cash's 'I Walk the Line.'"

The guitar is also the perfect instrument to play while singing. Try that with a trumpet! Also, musicians can play both chords and single notes with guitars. This allows them to play many types of music. Having a guitar is almost like having a portable orchestra.

Guitars allow musicians to express themselves. Musicians express themselves through their music. They also do this with their equipment. The look of a guitar can tell a lot about the style of its owner. Today, guitars are made in many different colors and shapes. There are even electric guitars that come in shapes like hearts and flowers.

Some guitar fans build their own guitars. They use different types of wood or other materials to make their guitars. Then they add color and images to their instruments.

There are guitar shows in every state. Collectors gather at these shows to learn more about guitars. There are Internet bulletin boards devoted to all the major brands and types of guitars. Bookstores are full of books and magazines on playing the guitar and collecting guitars. Music written for the guitar can be found on the Internet, in bookstores, or in music stores.

Today, a new generation of fans is playing the guitar. John Harrison is a middle-school teacher in Oregon. Harrison uses the guitar as a teaching tool. When his school cut music courses, Harrison started a guitar program.

The first year, there were only four guitars. This was not enough for all the students who wanted to play. Harrison asked people to donate guitars. The second year, he had enough guitars for 23 students. The third year, 41 students signed up. Soon, the guitar course was the second most popular class. Harrison has seen the guitar become a powerful motivator for the students. "I've seen friendships emerge from playing together," Harrison says. "I've seen kids focus, succeed, and become leaders in class."

"The most impressive result," Harrison adds, "is just witnessing the kids' awakenings that they're capable of expressing themselves in a positive way—a way that makes other people happy, too."

You can learn to play guitar, too!

Harrison's passion for guitar has rubbed off on his students. Here's what some of them say:

Alysssa: "I think it's great that so many diverse sounds and songs can be made with one instrument."

Emily: "You can never get bored. There are so many different styles and types of music you can play."

Katie: "If you're angry or sad or anything, you can play a song that lets your feelings out."

Chris: "The words that explain the guitar for me are *awesome*, *cool*, *expressive*, *emotional*, *happy*, *rock*, *jazzy*, *mellow*, *hip*, *out of the ordinary*."

Zoë: "It's super fun."

Reading what Harrison's students say proves that the guitar is likely to be popular for a long time to come. That probably sums it up as well as anything!

 Glossary

acoustic   played without electricity

amplifier   an electronic device that boosts the volume of an electric guitar's strings

auction   a sale in which people make bids, with the highest one being the winner

chords   three or more musical notes played at the same time

fingerboard   flat surface on the neck of the guitar that is pressed to make tones

frets   narrow ridges on the fingerboard

hollowbody   a guitar that has a large open chamber inside the body

luthier   someone who builds or repairs guitars

pickup   a magnet with coils of thin wire that acts like a microphone for the strings of an electric guitar

solidbody   a guitar built from one or more pieces of solid wood

soundhole   a round opening in the front of an acoustic guitar through which sound is projected

synthesizers   electric keyboards that can imitate the sounds of many instruments